# ASTEROIDS, METEORITES, AND COMETS

BY ARNOLD RINGSTAD

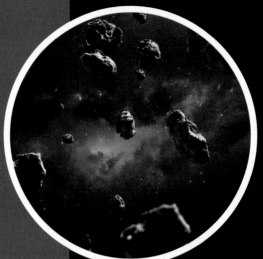

Published by The Child's World®
1980 Lookout Drive • Mankato, MN 56003-1705
800-599-READ • www.childsworld.com

Photographs ©: Marko Aliaksandr/Shutterstock
Images, cover, 1, 3; Vadim Sadovski/Shutterstock
Images, 2, 12; Lynette Cook/SOFIA/ARC/NASA, 4;
Red Line Editorial, 7 (background and planets);
Temstock/Shutterstock Images, 7 (comet);
Shutterstock Images, 8, 18; JPL-Caltech/UCLA/
MPS/DLR/IDA/NASA, 10; George Shelton/KSC/
NASA, 13; Siberian Art/Shutterstock Images, 14; P.
Jenniskens/SETI/ARC/NASA, 16, 17; Giotto Project/
ESA/JPL/NASA, 20; JSC/NASA, 21; JPL/NASA, 22

ISBN 9781503844780 (Reinforced Library Binding)
ISBN 9781503846135 (Portable Document Format)
ISBN 9781503847323 (Online Multi-user eBook)
LCCN 2019957688

Printed in the United States of America

**About the Author**
Arnold Ringstad loves reading
about space science and
exploration. He lives in Minnesota
with his wife and their cat.

# CONTENTS

# CHAPTER ONE

# WANDERING THROUGH SPACE

The **solar system** started as a huge cloud of dust and gas. **Gravity** pulled these materials together. About 4.5 billion years ago, these materials formed the sun and the planets. The sun is made up of burning gases. The planets are made up of rock and gas. Most of the material went into the sun and planets. But there was still some left over. This extra material formed asteroids and comets.

◄ Asteroids, meteorites, and comets are made of space materials that did not become planets.

Asteroids are pieces of rock. Comets are chunks of rock, dust, and frozen gas. Like the planets, these objects are in **orbit** around the sun. Most asteroids orbit in a circular path around the sun. Most comets orbit in long oval shapes. They spend most of their time far away from the sun, then they quickly swing close by it.

Asteroids and comets have not changed much since the solar system formed. Scientists are very interested in studying them. Asteroids and comets can show what the early solar system was like. This can give clues about how the planets formed, including Earth.

A comet's orbit is oval-shaped. Planets have a round orbit. ▶

# A COMET'S ORBIT

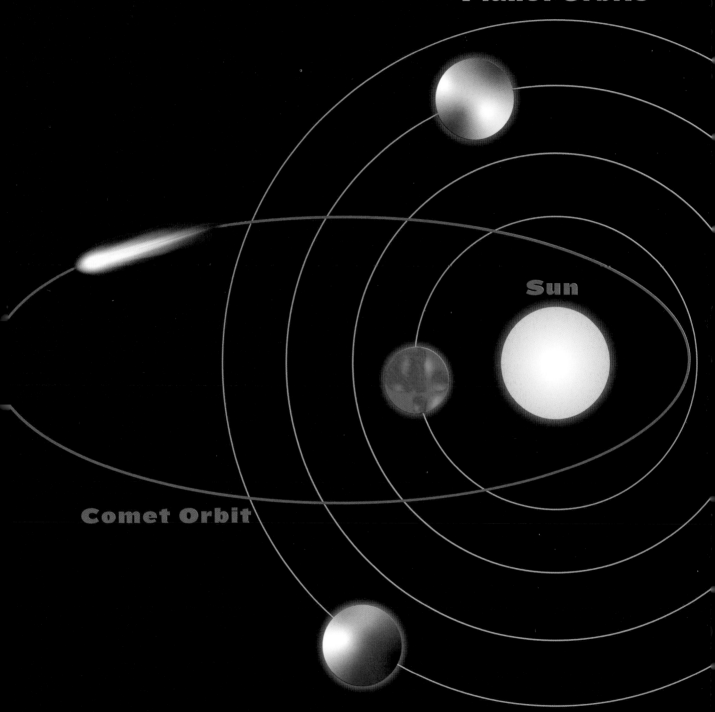

Planet Orbits

Sun

Comet Orbit

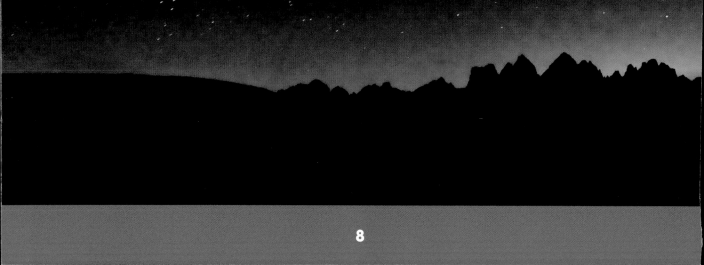

Space scientists have another reason to study asteroids and comets. These objects can be dangerous. Sometimes, asteroids and comets pass close to Earth. They can even hit our planet. When a piece of one of these objects hits a planet or moon, it is called a meteorite. A large meteorite hitting Earth could cause a lot of damage. Scientists study the orbits of asteroids and comets. They figure out if any are dangerous to Earth.

## DID YOU KNOW?

By February 2020, there were 932,209 known asteroids in the solar system. There were 3,608 known comets.

◄ Meteors burning in the sky can look beautiful from Earth. But if the meteors make it to Earth's surface as meteorites, they can cause serious damage.

Vesta is the
largest asteroid
in our solar system. A
spacecraft called *Dawn* took
this picture of Vesta in 2012.

## CHAPTER TWO

# ASTEROIDS

Most of the solar system's asteroids are in the asteroid belt. This is an area between Mars and Jupiter. Jupiter is the largest planet. It has very strong gravity. Sometimes, its gravity changes an asteroid's orbit. This sends the asteroid in a new direction. It may travel closer to the sun or farther away. It may even hit a planet, such as Earth.

Asteroids have many different sizes. The largest asteroid is called Vesta. It is located in the asteroid belt. Vesta is about 329 miles (530 km) across. Other asteroids are much smaller. They can be less than 33 feet (10 m) across.

**DID YOU KNOW?**

Put together, all the asteroids in the solar system have less **mass** than Earth's moon.

Asteroids come in all ► shapes and sizes.

Scientists can study asteroids from Earth. They send signals into space. The signals bounce off the asteroids. Scientists listen for the echoes. They can learn a lot from these echoes. They can learn how big an asteroid is and what its orbit looks like. They can even learn what kind of rock it is made of.

The spacecraft *Dawn* was launched in 2007. It collected information ► for scientists, such as information about Vesta's surface.

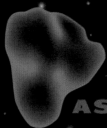

ASTEROID

COMET

METEOROID

METEOR

METEOR
SHOWER

METEORITE

# CHAPTER THREE

# METEORITES

Talking about meteorites can be confusing. There are a few different words that sound similar but mean different things. These words are *meteoroids*, *meteors*, and *meteorites*.

Meteoroids are pieces of rock or dust that are floating through space. They are usually pieces that have broken off from larger asteroids or comets. When a meteoroid enters a planet's **atmosphere**, it hits the atmosphere's gases at high speed. It starts to burn up. This burning piece of rock is a meteor. It glows brightly in the sky. People sometimes call meteors "shooting stars." Some meteors burn up completely. There is nothing left of them. But other meteors hit the ground. These are called meteorites.

◀ Meteoroids are pieces of rock in space. When meteoroids enter Earth's atmosphere, they become meteors. If a meteor hits Earth, it's called a meteorite.

▲
On October 7, 2008, an asteroid called 2008 TC3 entered Earth's atmosphere and became a meteor. Scientists and volunteers searched the desert of northern Sudan in Africa for meteorites.

Meteorite from asteroid 2008 TC3 ▶

Meteorites are dark in color. They have a burned surface that looks shiny. This forms when the meteorite passes through the atmosphere. The outside heats up. It melts and forms a shiny surface.

Compared to asteroids and comets, meteorites are easy to study. Scientists don't need to look in space. They can find meteorites on Earth and pick them up off the ground. Still, they can be tough to find. From a distance, meteorites look similar to normal rocks. There are some places where it is easier to see them. Meteorites can be spotted in deserts. They can also be seen in empty, icy places, such as Antarctica.

## DID YOU KNOW?

When a large meteorite hits a planet or moon, it leaves a big hole called a **crater**. Many craters can be seen on the moon. A few can be seen on Earth, too.

▲
Before people
understood comets, the
appearance of one was
usually taken as a bad sign.

18

# CHAPTER FOUR

# COMETS

Meteors shine brightly in the sky for a few moments. But comets put on a bigger show. Most of the time, comets are far from the sun. These cold chunks of frozen gas, rock, and dust drift through space. But eventually, their orbit brings them close to the sun. The sun's heat warms up the frozen gas. This gives the comet its own thin atmosphere. The sun's light pushes against some of the dust and gas. This forms a long, bright tail coming off the comet. A comet that comes close to Earth may be seen in the night sky for many days.

Many comets fly through the solar system on a regular schedule. For instance, Halley's Comet comes near Earth about every 75 years. It is named for scientist Edmond Halley. Halley studied records of comets appearing in the sky in 1456, 1531, 1607, and 1682. In 1705, he realized these were all the same comet. He predicted it would return in 1758. Halley did not live to see the comet. But he was correct.

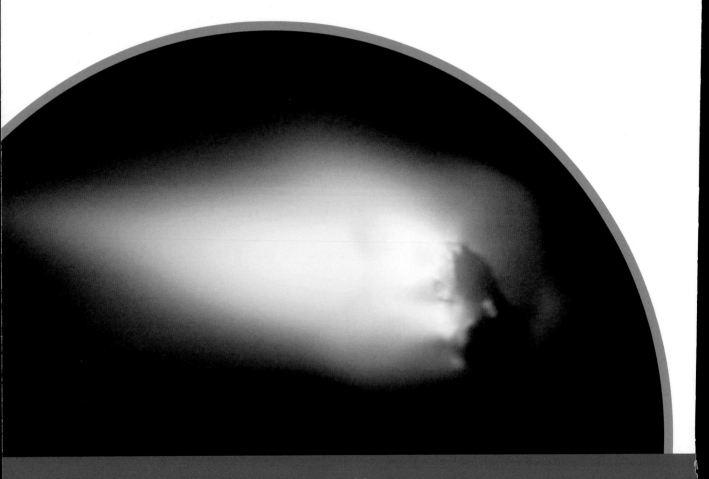

Another well-known comet is the ▶ Hale-Bopp comet. Astronauts on the space shuttle *Columbia* took this photo of the Hale-Bopp comet when it passed by Earth in 1997.

Scientists believe comets come from two main areas. The first is the Kuiper (KY-pur) Belt. This area is past the planet Neptune. It is named for scientist Gerard Kuiper. The comets from this area usually take less than 200 years to orbit the sun. The second area is the Oort cloud. This area is much farther away. Comets from this area can take up to 30 million years to orbit the sun.

Asteroids and comets can teach us a lot. Studying them reveals information about the early solar system. When pieces of them fall to Earth as meteorites, scientists can learn even more. These space objects are a window into the solar system's past.

◀ Spacecraft were able to take an up-close picture of Halley's Comet when it passed Earth in 1986.

# LOOKING INSIDE A COMET

The *Deep Impact* spacecraft launched from Earth in January 2005. A few months later, it arrived at a comet named Tempel 1. The spacecraft had an exciting mission. It released a smaller spacecraft called an impactor. The impactor was a heavy piece of metal. It carried small engines to steer itself.

The impactor smashed into Tempel 1. It made a huge flash of light and sent a giant cloud of material flying. This let *Deep Impact* look below the comet's surface. It was the first time people had ever looked inside a comet. The spacecraft sent pictures and information back to Earth. Scientists studied this information. They learned that the outside of the comet blocks heat from reaching the inside. This means that the deepest parts of the comet have probably not changed at all since the solar system formed.

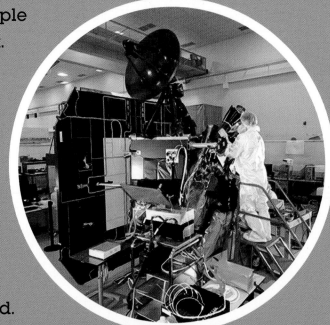

▲
*Deep Impact* was the first spacecraft to land on a comet.

# GLOSSARY

**atmosphere** (AT-muss-feer) An atmosphere is the layer of gases that surrounds a planet. When a meteoroid hits the atmosphere, it becomes a meteor.

**crater** (KRAY-tur) A crater is a large hole dug in the ground when rocks from space slam into a moon, planet, or dwarf planet. When a meteorite hits Earth, it can leave a crater.

**gravity** (GRAV-i-tee) Gravity is the force that pulls objects together. Jupiter's powerful gravity can change an asteroid's orbit.

**mass** (MASS) Mass is a measure of how much matter is in an object. Asteroids and comets make up a tiny part of the solar system's overall mass.

**orbit** (OR-bit) When an object is in orbit, it moves in a round path around another object. Asteroids and comets are in orbit around the sun.

**solar system** (SOH-ler SIS-tum) The solar system includes the sun and all the objects near it. Our solar system is home to thousands of asteroids and comets.

# TO LEARN MORE

## IN THE LIBRARY

Chiger, Arielle, and Adrienne Houk Maley. *20 Fun Facts about Asteroids and Comets*. New York, NY: Gareth Stevens Publishing, 2015.

Rathburn, Betsy. *Asteroids*. Minneapolis, MN: Bellwether Media, 2019.

Ringstad, Arnold. *Space Missions of the 21st Century*. Mankato, MN: The Child's World, 2016.

## ON THE WEB

Visit our website for links about asteroids, meteorites, and comets:

**childsworld.com/links**

*Note to Parents, Teachers, and Librarians: We routinely verify our Web links to make sure they are safe and active sites. So encourage your readers to check them out!*

# INDEX